8bjc

D0983020

12 REASONS TO LOVE
HOCKEY

by Phil Ervin

12 STORY LIBRARY

www.12StoryLibrary.com

12-Story Library is an imprint of Bookstaves and Press Room Editions

Produced for 12-Story Library by Red Line Editorial

Photographs ©: Joshua Sarner/Icon Sportswire/AP Images, cover, 1; George Grantham Bain Collection/ Library of Congress, 4; Kevork Djansezian/AP Images, 5; Al Messerschmidt/AP Images, 6; Skip Stewart/ AP Images, 7; Michael Tureski/Icon Sportswire/AP Images, 8; Foto011/Shutterstock Images, 9; Julio Cortez/AP Images, 10; A.E. Maloof/AP Images, 11; Iurii Osadchi/Shutterstock Images, 12; Chris O'Meara/AP Images, 13, 29; AP Images, 14, 15, 20; Sergei Bachlakov/Shutterstock Images, 16; Andy Blenkush/Cal Sport Media/AP Images, 17; Adwo/Shutterstock Images, 18; Joseph Sohm/Shutterstock Images, 19; John Crouch/Icon Sportswire/AP Images, 21; iofoto/Shutterstock Images, 22; Tom Pidgeon/ AP Images, 23; David Kirouac/Icon Sportswire/AP Images, 24, 28; Govorov Pavel/Shutterstock Images, 26; meunierd/Shutterstock Images, 27

Library of Congress Cataloging-in-Publication Data
Names: Ervin, Phil, author.
Title: 12 reasons to love hockey / by Phil Ervin.
Other titles: Twelve reasons to love hockey
Description: Mankato, Minnesota : 12 Story Library, 2018. | Series: Sports
    report | Includes bibliographical references and index. | Audience: Grade
    4 to 6.
Identifiers: LCCN 2016047144 (print) | LCCN 2016053836 (ebook) | ISBN
    9781632354280 (hardcover : alk. paper) | ISBN 9781632354976 (pbk. : alk.
    paper) | ISBN 9781621435495 (hosted e-book)
Subjects: LCSH: Hockey--Juvenile literature.
Classification: LCC GV847.25 E78 2018 (print) | LCC GV847.25 (ebook) | DDC
    796.962--dc23
LC record available at https://lccn.loc.gov/2016047144

Printed in China
022017

Access free, up-to-date content on this topic plus a full digital version of this book. Scan the QR code on page 31 or use your school's login at 12StoryLibrary.com.

Table of Contents

Hockey Has Special Stories

Hockey is an exciting sport played around the world. It's especially important in Canada. Many great hockey tales come from Canada. The first official game of indoor ice hockey was played March 3, 1875, in Montreal, Quebec.

However, research suggests the sport was first played in Britain. It dates back as far as the 1790s there. There are even stories of British princes and kings playing hockey.

The sport has changed in some ways since it was first played in Britain. But both then and now, hockey is full of amazing stories. Every player in the National Hockey League (NHL) has tales to tell.

There are many stories from women's hockey, too. The women's

Amateur hockey team in New York in 1911

Thanks to the Olympics, women's hockey has boomed.

game has seen a surge in popularity since the 1990s. The Olympics have been especially exciting. More and more women and girls are playing the sport.

All players have stories about the dedication it takes to reach the highest level of the sport. Players remember hours of practice over the years.

Fans have stories of their own. They remember special moments that make them love the game. Many fans will never forget when their team won a Stanley Cup or championship. Other fans will never forget when their team lost a big game. Win or lose, hockey is full of stories.

31

Number of NHL teams as of the 2017–18 season, when Las Vegas joined the league.

- Hockey is enjoyed around the world and especially in Canada.
- Hockey was first played in Britain.
- Women's hockey has been rising in popularity since the 1990s.
- Players and fans have favorite stories.

THINK ABOUT IT

What was the first time you remember watching or playing hockey? What great stories do you recall?

5

Nicknames Make Hockey Fun

Wayne Gretzky is considered the best hockey player ever. He's known as the Great One. He's one of many NHL players with a nickname. These names make hockey fun. It makes the players memorable for fans.

Most young hockey fans grow up idolizing NHL players. Young Gretzky did, too. Gordie Howe was Gretzky's favorite. Howe had a nickname as well. He was known as Mr. Hockey.

Sidney Crosby is also considered one of hockey's best. He's called Sid the Kid. He first played hockey when he was three years old. As he grew up, he spent hours shooting pucks at his family's dryer. He joined the Pittsburgh Penguins at age 18. In 2016, he won his second Stanley Cup with the Penguins.

Angela Ruggiero is considered one of the best US women's hockey players. She has had a few nicknames throughout her

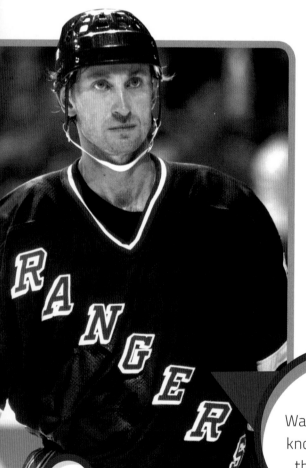

Wayne Gretzky is known simply as the Great One.

9

Times Gretzky won the Hart Memorial Trophy as the NHL's most valuable player.

- Many hockey players have fun nicknames.
- Gretzky is the Great One, and Gordie Howe is Mr. Hockey.
- Angela Ruggiero had many nicknames.

career. In youth leagues against boys, she was known as the Terminator. In college, she was Rugger. Later, when she appeared on *The Apprentice* television show, she was called the Olympian. That's because she won four medals in four Olympics. In 1998, she won gold with Team USA.

Angela Ruggiero was inducted into hockey's Hall of Fame in 2015.

Goalies also have cool nicknames. Patrick Roy is known as Saint Patrick. He was one of the best goalies of all time. He played for the Montreal Canadiens and Colorado Avalanche. Dominik Hašek played most of his years with the Buffalo Sabres and Detroit Red Wings. He was so good, he was called the Dominator.

Great Teams Make Great Hockey

The NHL has 31 teams. The league is divided into two conferences. The Eastern Conference has 16 teams. The Western Conference has 15 teams. Each conference has two divisions. The top three teams from each division make the Stanley Cup Playoffs. Two other teams from each conference also make the playoffs. Those are known as wild card teams.

The National Women's Hockey League (NWHL) began in 2015. As of 2016, it had four teams: the Boston Pride, Buffalo Beauts, Connecticut Whale, and New York Riveters. The Boston Pride were champions in the league's first season.

There are many great teams outside professional hockey. There are 60 National Collegiate

The Boston Pride is one of four teams in the NWHL.

WORLDWIDE TEAMS

There are many hockey leagues outside the United States and Canada. Russia's Kontinental Hockey League (KHL) is considered the world's best league after the NHL.

Athletic Association (NCAA) Division I men's teams. Division I women's hockey has 36 teams. The NCAA tournaments decide the national champions.

Each NHL team has two minor league teams. Players develop their skills in the minors before moving up to the NHL. The East Coast Hockey League is for entry-level players. The American Hockey League is one step away from the NHL.

2013

First year wild card teams were used in the NHL playoffs.

- The NHL has 31 teams divided into two conferences.
- The NWHL has four teams.
- Youth hockey starts around age six.

High school hockey is very popular in some places. In Minnesota, for example, the state high school hockey tournament draws thousands of fans each year. At the youngest level, youth hockey starts around age six. It's divided into mite, squirt, peewee, and bantam leagues.

Youth hockey begins with mite leagues.

9

Goals Light the Lamp

There's nothing quite like a goal in hockey. A light behind the goalie blinks red. Fans call that "lighting the lamp." Loud music often plays. And the home fans go nuts. Some goals win games. Some win championships. Others win gold medals.

Former Boston Bruins defenseman Bobby Orr scored what many consider the most famous goal in history. It came in Game 4 of the 1970 Stanley Cup Final. The Bruins went to overtime against the St. Louis Blues. Orr got tripped as he shot, but he knew it was a goal. He

Sidney Crosby scores the goal that won gold for Team Canada in 2010.

flew through the air with his arms outstretched in celebration. With his goal, Boston won the Stanley Cup.

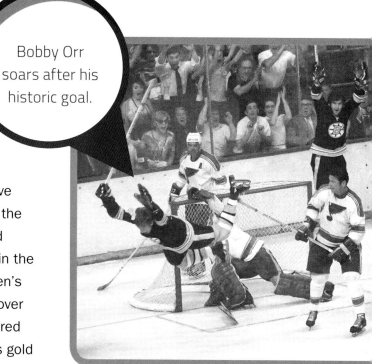

Bobby Orr soars after his historic goal.

Some of the biggest goals have happened in the Olympics. At the 2002 Olympics, Jayna Hefford scored with two seconds left in the game. The goal won the women's gold medal for Team Canada over Team USA. Sidney Crosby scored in overtime in the 2010 men's gold medal game. That sealed the win for Team Canada over Team USA.

There have also been some incredible college hockey goals. Tyler McGregor scored in overtime in the 2006 NCAA tournament. His Holy Cross team upset the favored Minnesota.

53
Seconds into overtime when Tyler McGregor scored in the 2006 NCAA championship.

- Bobby Orr's 1970 Stanley Cup goal may be the most famous NHL goal.
- Jayna Hefford and Sidney Crosby scored winning goals in the Olympics.
- There have been incredible goals in college hockey as well.

50 GOALS

Sometimes great goals come one after another. In the 1944–45 season, Maurice Richard had 50 goals in 50 games. He played for the Montreal Canadiens. He was known as the Rocket.

Hockey Has Exciting Action

Hockey is one of the fastest sports. Players can skate more than 20 miles per hour (32.1 km/h). And slap shots can travel more than 100 miles per hour (160.9 km/h). It's fast-paced action.

Players use up a lot of energy on the ice. That's why they work in shifts. They play for a short period, usually less than a minute, and then they come out to rest. Players can change shifts at any time. The game doesn't need to stop. Each shift includes three forwards. These are players focused on offense. Many times, the same forwards play in all shifts together. These groupings are called lines. Two defensemen also go out each shift.

Players spend a lot of time training and practicing. Practices include drills for stickhandling, passing, and shooting. Teammates often play practice games against one another.

Games are usually divided into three periods.

Resting in between short shifts allows players to work hard when they're on the ice.

4

Number of lines on NHL teams.

- Hockey is one of the world's fastest sports.
- Players are on the ice in shifts.
- Hockey games are usually divided into three periods.

THINK ABOUT IT

Why do you think it's important for hockey players to train and practice? How do you think linemates learn to work together?

Each is 20 minutes long. In the NHL, games that are tied after three periods go to overtime. In overtime, teams play with only three players, plus goalies. Fewer players on the ice leads to better scoring chances. A regular-season game goes to a shootout if no one scores in the five-minute overtime. Playoff games go to sudden-death overtime. This means the first team to score wins.

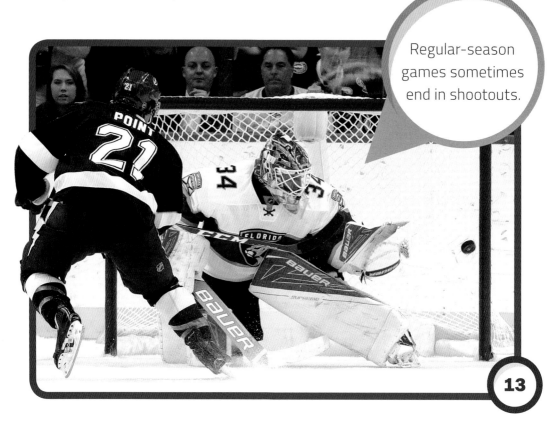

Regular-season games sometimes end in shootouts.

Hockey's "Miracle" Inspired a Nation

Tensions were high before the 1980 Olympics. It was a difficult time in US history. Jobs and money were scarce. Also, the United States and the Soviet Union were in a Cold War (1947–1991). The two nations did not actually fight any battles. Instead, they threatened each other with nuclear war. Both countries wanted to be the world's superpower.

Team USA celebrates the "Miracle on Ice."

12

Number of Team USA players, out of 20, who were from Minnesota, as was Brooks.

- The 1980 "Miracle on Ice" is a great moment in sports history.
- Herb Brooks coached the team.
- After beating the Soviet Union, Team USA beat Finland for the gold medal.

Coach Herb Brooks led the team to victory.

Led by coach Herb Brooks, the US men's hockey team faced the Soviet Union in the semifinal round of the Olympics. The winner would have the inside track on the gold medal. Team USA was not expected to win. The Soviet Union had won four straight

TEAM CANADA

In recent years, Team Canada has been as good as gold at the Olympics. The Canadian men's team won gold in 2010 and 2014. And the Canadian women's team claimed its fourth straight gold in 2014.

gold medals. The US hadn't won gold since 1960.

The teams battled it out. The game was tied 3–3 in the third period. Then US captain Mike Eruzione scored. Team USA led 4–3. The final minutes were tense. Goalie Jim Craig made several great saves. Team USA held on for the win.

"Do you believe in miracles? Yes!" sportscaster Al Michaels shouted. It was a giant upset. The game became known as the "Miracle on Ice."

Team USA went on to beat Finland to earn the gold medal. Team USA lifted spirits as Americans celebrated the victories.

Fans Support Their Teams

Nothing compares to the excitement of a packed hockey game. Fans wear their favorite players' jerseys. The entire arena is filled with noise. Fans throw hats onto the ice when there's a hat trick. That's when a player scores three goals in a game.

Hockey fans are passionate about their teams. Many NHL teams play in front of sold-out crowds for nearly every home game. Chicago Blackhawks fans are regarded as some of the best. So are fans for the Montreal Canadiens, Boston Bruins, and Minnesota Wild. The sport of hockey is very big in these communities. A few teams see sold-out crowds even for away games.

Hockey was once only popular in places with cold winters. Now

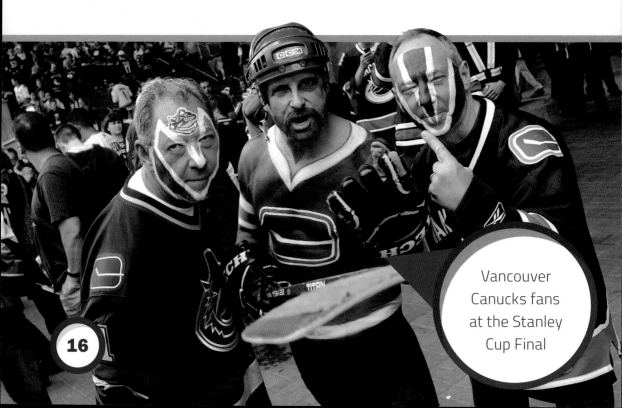

Vancouver Canucks fans at the Stanley Cup Final

6

Number of national championships the University of Minnesota women's team won in 12 years.

- Hockey fans are passionate.
- Many NHL teams sell out every game.
- Hockey is popular even in some warm-weather communities.
- Fans love college hockey as well.

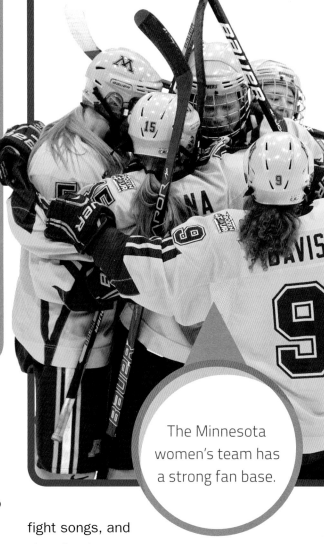

The Minnesota women's team has a strong fan base.

there are many NHL teams in warm-weather states and cities. They include the Tampa Bay Lightning, Dallas Stars, and Los Angeles Kings. All three teams have strong fan bases. All three have also won Stanley Cups.

When teams win, fans love to celebrate with them. When teams win the Stanley Cup, cities often throw big parades. In 2013, 2 million people went to the parade for the Chicago Blackhawks.

College hockey also has great fans. College games have a fun feel. Many games feature pep bands, fight songs, and cheerleaders. This pumps up the crowd. The Universities of North Dakota, Wisconsin, and Minnesota rank highest in attendance for college men's hockey. Minnesota and Wisconsin are two of the most popular college women's teams.

Everyone Dreams of the Cup

Every NHL player dreams of lifting the Stanley Cup. The cup is the trophy given to the NHL champions.

The cup has a long history. Lord Stanley of Preston was the governor general of Canada. He gave the cup to a hockey club in 1892. The NHL began using it as its championship trophy in 1926. It's the oldest trophy in major professional sports. It's also one of the heaviest. The cup weighs 34.5 pounds (15.6 kg).

At the end of the Stanley Cup Final, the winning team's captain gets the cup first. Then he passes it on. Each player takes his turn skating with the cup. That summer, each player gets the trophy for a day. He can take it wherever he wants.

Many great players have won the cup more than once. This list includes Wayne Gretzky, Gordie Howe, and Sidney Crosby. Many players never win it. For those who do, it's a special moment.

Ray Bourque played for the Boston Bruins for nearly 21 seasons. At the end of his 21st season, he was traded to the Colorado Avalanche. It was

Players from the winning team have their names engraved on the Stanley Cup.

in hopes of his finally winning the cup. In his 22nd and final season, Bourque got to kiss the Stanley Cup.

NHL teams are proud of their Stanley Cup wins. The Montreal Canadiens have won the most cups with 23. They have 10 more cups than the next team, the Toronto Maple Leafs.

5

Stanley Cups the Edmonton Oilers won from 1984 to 1990.

- The Stanley Cup is the trophy for the NHL championship.
- The cup is the oldest trophy in major professional sports.
- Ray Bourque won the cup in his 22nd season.

Each winning player gets a special day with the cup.

Goalies Make Incredible Saves

A slap shot blasts toward the net. Fans wait for the red light to flash. But no. The goalie made a terrific save.

Goalies, or goaltenders, guard the net and try to stop goals. They have to be great athletes. They must be quick. Pucks fly in at incredible speeds. Goalies also have to be flexible. Sometimes to stop a puck, goalies must do splits. And goalies have to be good skaters.

Jacques Plante started wearing a mask after a puck broke his nose.

THINK ABOUT IT

If you were a hockey goalie, what would you paint on your mask? Why?

18

Number of games the Canadiens won in a row after Jacques Plante wore his mask.

- Hockey goalies are great athletes.
- Goalie masks have changed over the years.
- Many goalies have special designs on their masks.

They must be able to slide and shuffle. Players shoot from every angle, trying to get the puck past.

Goalies wear special masks for protection. The masks have changed over the years. For many years, goalies didn't wear masks at all. Then in 1959, a puck hit Canadiens goalie Jacques Plante in the face. He returned to the game with a simple fiberglass mask. After that, goalies began wearing masks more often. In 1968, Bruins goalie Gerry Cheevers painted stitches on his mask to show what his face would look like if he didn't have a mask. That began a trend of decorating the masks.

Robin Lehner's mask pays tribute to the US armed forces.

Today, goalies wear special masks that are built into helmets. There's also a piece that protects the neck. Each mask has a unique design. Some designs tie in with the goalies' nicknames. Eddie "the Eagle" Belfour had eagles painted on his helmet.

Coaches Lead the Way

10

Hockey coaches must be great leaders. They must also make quick decisions. It's not an easy job.

Coaches are responsible for creating lines. They also put together defensive pairings. They decide what plays might work best. Coaches then share the plans with the players. The team counts on the coach's direction.

But there's more to being a coach. Coaching is mostly about people skills. Coaches need good relationships with the players. The team needs to trust the coach. Coaches must also have good relationships with other people who work for the team. In the NHL, this includes the general manager. The general manager's job is to build the team's roster. The coach's job is to get that roster to win.

Scotty Bowman is the winningest coach in NHL history. He coached many teams. He's perhaps most remembered as the

> A coach must earn the players' trust.

coach for the Detroit Red Wings. Current Blackhawks coach Joel Quenneville has the second-most wins in NHL history.

There are some successful coaches in college hockey, too. Bill Mandigo of Middlebury College is the winningest women's college hockey coach. He led the team to three NCAA Division III titles. In Division I women's hockey, Katey Stone of Harvard has the most wins.

Jerry York has the most wins for NCAA Division I men's hockey. He currently coaches Boston College. He has coached five national

1

Number of coaches who have won a Stanley Cup, an Olympic gold medal, and a World Championship: Mike Babcock.

- Coaching is not an easy job.
- Coaching is about relationships.
- Scotty Bowman has more wins than any other NHL coach.

championship teams. Part of his success comes from keeping a positive attitude.

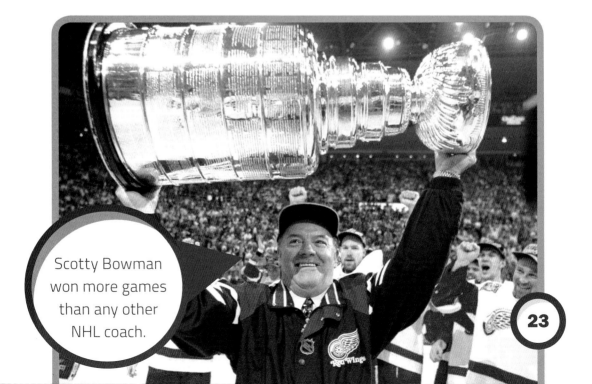

Scotty Bowman won more games than any other NHL coach.

23

11

Hockey Jerseys Are Memorable

Usually, hockey players aren't the only ones at the rink wearing jerseys. Fans often wear the jerseys of their favorite teams or

players. Jerseys are an important part of hockey culture.

Some jerseys haven't changed in years. The Canadiens have worn essentially the same jerseys for

The Canadiens jersey is a favorite in the NHL.

24

- Hockey jerseys are popular with fans.
- The Original Six jerseys are famous.
- Other jerseys have more flair with animal themes.

decades. They are red, blue, and white. They feature a *C* logo with an *H* in the middle. The *C* stands for Canadiens. The *H* stands for hockey.

The Canadiens are an Original Six team. The Original Six are the oldest teams in the NHL. The other teams are the Chicago Blackhawks, New York Rangers, Philadelphia Flyers, Toronto Maple Leafs, and Detroit Red Wings. These teams are full of history. The Original Six teams all have memorable jerseys. For example, the Maple Leafs jersey is blue with a white leaf. The team began in 1927. The jersey has changed very little since then.

Some jerseys are more creative. This is especially true for newer teams. The Florida Panthers and Nashville Predators have exciting jerseys with animals. The Minnesota Wild's jersey also has an animal design. The logo is shaped like a wild animal's head. The NWHL has jerseys with animal themes as well. The Boston Pride logo features claw marks.

SWEATERS

Many players, coaches, and fans call jerseys "sweaters." In the early days of hockey, players wore thick, sweater-like shirts during games. This helped them stay warm, especially when playing outdoors. Today's hockey jerseys are lighter and thinner.

Hockey Has Great Rinks

From Gretzky to Crosby, nearly every hockey player grew up playing on a special rink. Some players skated on frozen ponds or lakes. Other players skated in their own backyards. In the northern United States and Canada, some families flood their yards in winter. This creates a perfect sheet of ice. The Granato family had a backyard rink. Cammi Granato went on to become a US Olympic hero. Her brother Tony played in the NHL.

Other players grew up playing on indoor rinks. This includes the growing number of players from warmer climates. Some NHL players come from places where it's hard to

Frozen ponds and lakes make great hockey rinks.

have a backyard rink. Auston Matthews joined the Maple Leafs in 2016 as the top pick in the draft. He grew up in Scottsdale, Arizona.

When it comes to indoor rinks, the NHL has great arenas. Montreal's Bell Centre is among the top. It's the largest arena in the league. Still, nearly every game is sold out.

The University of North Dakota's Ralph Engelstad Arena is considered the best in college hockey. In fact, some consider it one of the best hockey arenas at any level. It has many features typically seen only in NHL arenas.

Montreal's Bell Centre is considered one of the best arenas.

OUTDOOR HOCKEY

Most hockey players have fond memories of outdoor games. In recent years, the NHL and NCAA have held outdoor games in this tradition. These games usually take place in large stadiums. The NHL's Winter Classic and Stadium Series games are outside.

21,287
Number of seats in the Bell Centre for a hockey game.

- Many hockey players played on a special rink growing up.
- More players now come from warm-weather states.
- There are great arenas in the NHL and NCAA.

27

Fact Sheet

- Five skaters are on the ice at a time: a center, a left wing, a right wing, and two defensemen. When both teams have five skaters on the ice, it's called even strength.

- When a player commits a penalty, he or she must sit in the penalty box for a certain amount of time. That team is then shorthanded during the penalty. Teams go on the power play when their opponent is shorthanded.

- The International Ice Hockey Federation oversees hockey worldwide. It hosts a variety of international men's and women's tournaments, including the Olympics.

- Union College is in New York. Its men's hockey team won the 2014 NCAA Division I national championship. The Dutchmen did it even though their school doesn't award athletic scholarships.

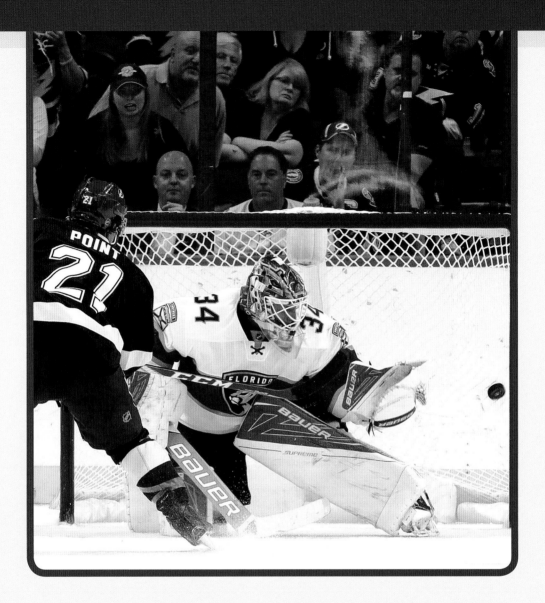

- As a kid, Wayne Gretzky once sent his hero, Gordie Howe, a letter. Howe mailed him back a signed picture of himself. Howe later came to Gretzky's hometown of Brantford, Ontario. The two met and took a picture together. Gretzky was about 10 years old.

- The United States won the first Olympic gold medal in women's hockey in 1998 in Nagano, Japan. Canada then won the next four gold medals, beating Team USA in the final game three times.

Glossary

attendance
The number of people who go to a game.

defense
In sports, an action meant to protect a team or prevent the other team from scoring.

drill
A physical or mental exercise that builds skill through regular practice.

flexible
Able to bend and stretch easily.

league
A collection of teams that compete against each other.

offense
In sports, an action meant to help a team score.

roster
The list of players on a team.

slap shot
A hard long-range shot made with a swinging stroke.

sudden death
An overtime format where the first team to score wins.

tournament
A competition in which teams who lose get knocked out.

tradition
A pattern or set way of doing something over time.

upset
When the team favored to win loses.

For More Information

Books

Burgan, Michael. *Miracle on Ice: How a Stunning Upset United a Country.* North Mankato, MN: Compass Point, 2016.

Herman, Gail. *Who Is Wayne Gretzky?* New York: Grosset & Dunlap, 2015.

Kwak, Sarah. *Face-Off: Top 10 Lists of Everything in Hockey.* New York: Sports Illustrated, 2015.

Visit 12StoryLibrary.com

Scan the code or use your school's login at **12StoryLibrary.com** for recent updates about this topic and a full digital version of this book. Enjoy free access to:

- Digital ebook
- Breaking news updates
- Live content feeds
- Videos, interactive maps, and graphics
- Additional web resources

Note to educators: Visit 12StoryLibrary.com/register to sign up for free premium website access. Enjoy live content plus a full digital version of every 12-Story Library book you own for every student at your school.

Index

Bourque, Ray, 18–19
Bowman, Scotty, 22–23
Brooks, Herb, 15

Canada, 4, 5, 9, 11, 15, 18, 26
Cheevers, Gerry, 21
coaches, 15, 22–23, 25
college hockey, 8–9, 11, 17, 23, 27
Crosby, Sidney, 6, 11, 18, 26

fans, 5, 6, 9, 10, 16–17, 20, 24, 25

goalies, 7, 10, 13, 15, 20–21
Granato, Cammi, 26
Granato, Tony, 26
Gretzky, Wayne, 6, 7, 18, 26

Hašek, Dominik, 7
Hefford, Jayna, 11
Howe, Gordie, 6, 7, 18

jerseys, 16, 24–25

Mandigo, Bill, 23
Matthews, Auston, 27
McGregor, Tyler, 11
Miracle on Ice, 14–15

National Hockey League (NHL), 4, 5, 6, 7, 8, 9, 11, 12, 13, 16, 17, 18–19, 22, 23, 25, 26, 27
National Women's Hockey League (NWHL), 8, 25

Olympics, 5, 7, 11, 14–15, 23, 26
Original Six, 25

Orr, Bobby, 10–11
overtime, 10, 11, 13

Plante, Jacques, 21

Quenneville, Joel, 23

rinks, 26–27
Roy, Patrick, 7
Ruggiero, Angela, 6–7

Stanley Cup, 5, 6, 8, 10, 11, 17, 18–19, 23
Stone, Katey, 23

York, Jerry, 23
youth hockey, 9

About the Author

Phil Ervin was born and raised in Omaha, Nebraska. He has written five other children's sports books. Phil has worked as a reporter for Fox Sports and the Minnesota Wild.

READ MORE FROM 12-STORY LIBRARY

Every 12-Story Library book is available in many formats. For more information, visit 12StoryLibrary.com.